Friends

M000206495

words by Joelie Croser
photographs by Nigel Croser

I have a friend.

We talk and laugh.

We walk to school together.

We play games together.

We share food.

We share toys.

We share books.

We share clothes, sometimes.

He comes to my house.

I go in his car.

We make things together.

We watch TV together.

We have fun.

He is my friend.

I am his friend too.